DINOSAURS!

by
Kathy Wilmore

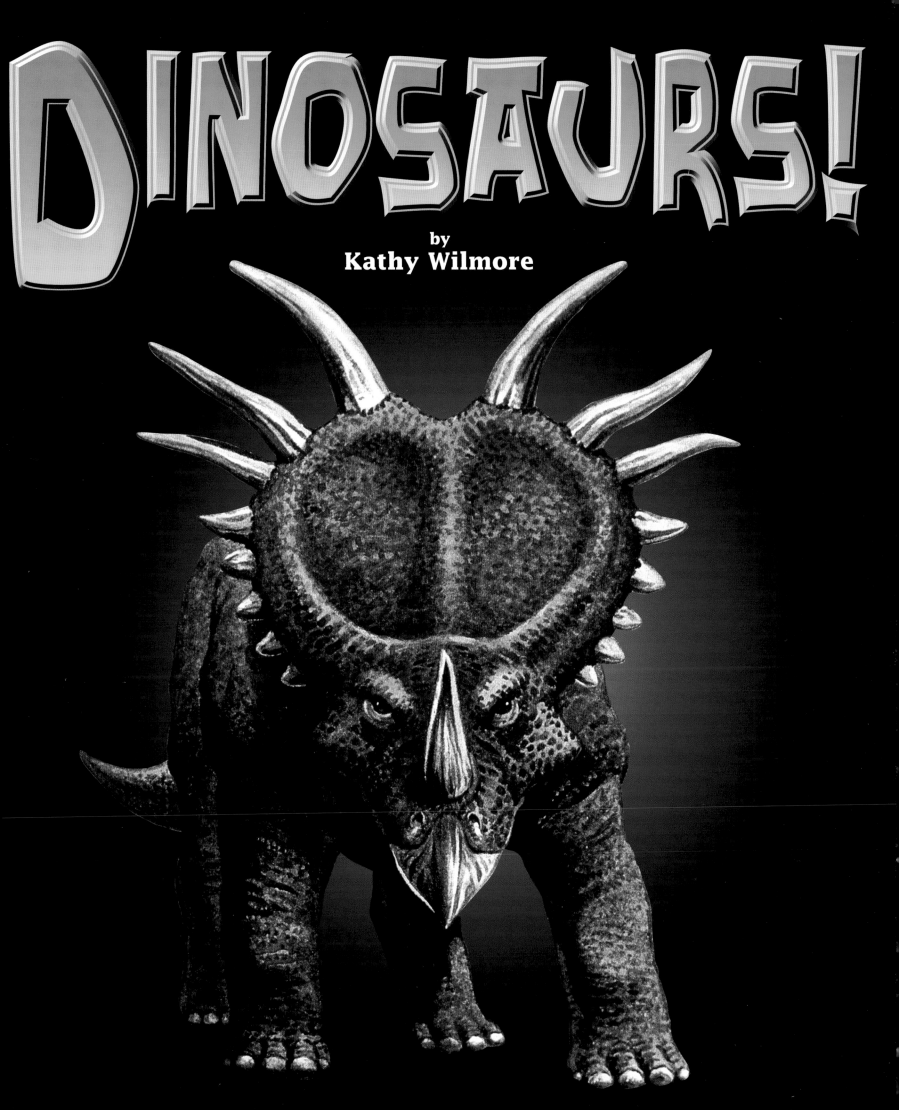

Consultant:

Carl Mehling
Collections Manager for Fossil Amphibians,
Reptiles, and Birds
Division of Paleontology
American Museum of Natural History
New York, New York

Picture Credits

AP/Wide World: pp. 39 (fossil), 44-45 (*Barosaurus* skeleton and *Barosaurus* painting)

François Gohier: pp. 22 (*Archaeopteryx*), 30-31 (*Triceratops* skeleton, *Triceratops* model, & *Protoceratops*), 42 (boy with skull), 45 (*Coelophysis* fossil)

Natural History Museum (London): pp. 15 (skull), 16-17 (*Kentrosaurus*), 18-19 (*Allosaurus*), 21 (*Megalosaurus*), 23 (*Confuciusornis*), 25, 26, 29 (both), 31 (*Styracosaurus*), 42 (top), 43

Natural History Museum/J. Sibbick: pp. 22-23 (series), 24-25 (hadrosaurs herd), 37

National History Museum/Orbis: pp. 4-5, 6-7 (all), 8-9 (both), 10, 12, 13 (*Seismosaurus*), 14, 17 (*Tuojiangosaurus*), 18 (*Cryolophosaurus*), 19 (*Elaphrosaurus*), 20-21 (*Dilophosaurus*), 27 (both), 28, 30, 31 (both), 32-33 (both), 36 (both), 38 (both), 40-41 (both), 48

Visit us at **www.kidsbooks.com**®

CONTENTS

INTRODUCTION

Are you fascinated by dinosaurs? If so, you are not alone. Dinosaurs have captured the interest of generations of humans—ever since experts began studying huge bone fossils found in the early 19th century. In 1842, scientist Richard Owen came up with the name *dinosaur* from two Greek words: *deinos*, meaning "terrible," and *sauros*, meaning "lizard." Since then, experts have learned a great deal about dinosaurs. You will, too, when you read this book.

How We Know

How do we know so much about dinosaurs? Scientists study fossils. A *fossil* is any evidence of ancient living things that have been naturally preserved. Fossils are not just bones. They can be many things, including teeth, wood, shells, and footprints. They can even be the faintest impressions of skin, feathers, or leaves.

Dinosaur Times

Dinosaurs have lived on Earth for an amazingly long time—more than 200 million years. You may know that most dinosaurs died out about 65 million years ago (MYA), but did you know that some are still with us? You see them every day. Many experts consider birds to be dinosaurs.

Most dinosaurs lived during a time known as the Age of Reptiles. Scientists call it the Mesozoic (meh-zuh-ZOH-ik) Era. They divide it into three periods—the Cretaceous (krih-TAY-shus), the Jurassic (ju-RAS-ik), and the Triassic (try-AS-ik). Important changes took place during each period. The chart below tells you more.

Dinosaurs were not the only animals on Earth during those times. Pterosaurs (TER-oh-sores), which you will meet on pages 10–11, lived then, too. So did many other kinds of reptiles, as well as mammals, amphibians, and other animals.

ERA	PERIOD*	YEARS AGO**	AGE	IMPORTANT EVENTS
MESOZOIC	Cretaceous	144 to 65 MYA	AGE OF REPTILES	Many new, exotic dinosaur forms arise. The first flowering plants appear. At the end of this period, nonbird dinosaurs, pterosaurs, marine reptiles, and many other animals and plants become extinct (die out).
	Jurassic	206 to 144 MYA		Pliosaurs (PLY-oh-sores) appear. The pliosaur was a large marine reptile with a large head and short neck. Dinosaurs roam the land. Mammals remain small. The first birds appear.
	Triassic	251 to 206 MYA		The first dinosaurs appear, along with frogs, turtles, crocodiles, pterosaurs, and the first mammals. Plesiosaurs (PLEE-zee-oh-sores) appear. This was a type of large marine reptile with flippers.

*listed from most recent to farther back • **MYA = million years ago

4

About This Book

When you look through this book, you will see a band along the top of each page.

On the left side is a title that tells you something about the dinosaurs on those two pages. For instance, many are labeled *Meat-eaters* or *Plant-eaters*. Experts often put dinosaurs in one of those categories. Other titles tell you something else about the dinosaurs—a description, such as *Giants*, or a group name, such as *Hadrosaurs*.

On the right side, you will see a heading telling you when the dinosaurs on those two pages lived. Some dinosaurs lived in just one of the three periods. Others lived during two or three of the periods.

Keep in Mind

The dinosaurs in this book are nonbird dinosaurs that are now extinct. Bird dinosaurs have been around since the Jurassic Period.

Are you ready to explore the wonderful world of dinosaurs? Then what are you waiting for? Turn the page!

PLANT-EATERS

Early Riser ▶

The largest of the known early plant-eaters, *Melanorosaurus* (muh-LAN-oh-roh-SORE-us) was 40 feet long. It had a small head and a long neck that enabled it to reach treetops for food as it stood on all fours. Thick, elephantlike legs supported the huge, heavy body. Fossils of this dinosaur were found in South Africa's Black Mountain region. That is what gave this giant its name—*Melanorosaurus* means "Black Mountain lizard."

◀ All Grown Up?

Mussaurus (muh-SORE-us) means "mouse lizard," a name that fits. *Mussaurus* was one of the smallest dinosaur fossils ever found. Skeletons of this animal, found in Argentina, were only eight inches long, with a one-inch-long skull. Those skeletons belonged to babies, but the adults probably were small, too—perhaps ten feet long. *Mussaurus* lived about 215 million years ago.

Quick-escape Artist ▶

Pisanosaurus (pye-SAN-uh-SORE-us) lived about 225 million years ago. *Pisanosaurus* probably stood on two legs and was a fast runner. This plant-eater didn't have to be fast to get food. It had to be fast to avoid becoming food—for larger meat-eating dinosaurs.

7

MEAT-EATERS

▲ Swift and Sharp

This dinosaur's three-foot-long body was built for speed. After running down its prey, *Eoraptor* (EE-oh-RAP-tur) could grab hold with its sharp-clawed fingers, then chomp down with its sharp teeth. *Eoraptor*, whose name means "dawn grasper," is one of the earliest dinosaurs known.

▼ Cannibal Animal?

More than 100 *Coelophysis* (SEEL-uh-FYE-sis) skeletons have been found in New Mexico with the bones of smaller *Coelophysis* among their ribs. Were the little ones inside the big ones' stomach? Did this dinosaur eat its own kind? Scientists used to think so, but now that they are studying fossils found more recently, they are reconsidering their theories.

▲ Bony Evidence

Parts of *Staurikosaurus* (STAW-ri-kuh-SORE-us) skeletons have been found in Brazil. Judging by those bones, experts believe that this dinosaur was about seven feet long, had long jaws and a slender body, and ran on two legs.

▲ Buggin' Out

Although its name means "leaping foot," *Saltopus* (SAWL-toh-pus) used its strong, lean legs for running. *Saltopus* probably fed mostly on insects. Its hollow bones kept it light in weight—about two pounds. This swift hunter was about the size of a modern-day housecat, but ran on two legs, not four.

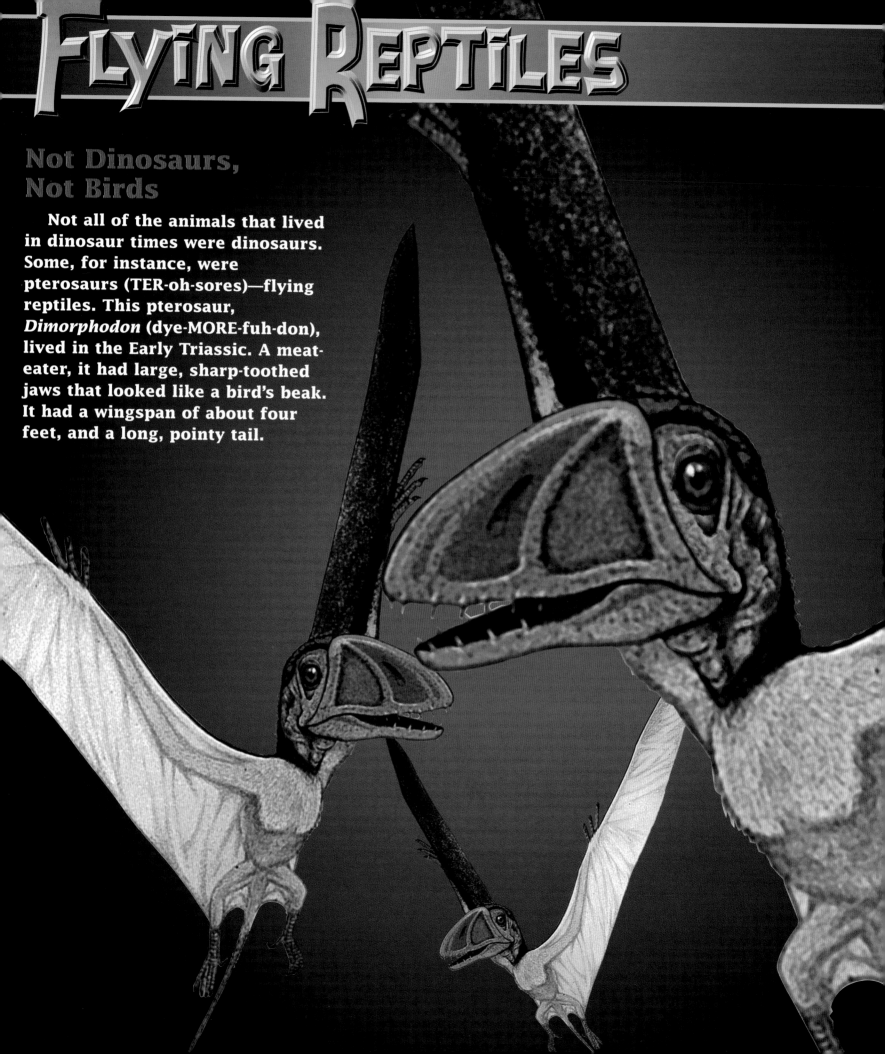

FLYING REPTILES

Not Dinosaurs, Not Birds

Not all of the animals that lived in dinosaur times were dinosaurs. Some, for instance, were pterosaurs (TER-oh-sores)—flying reptiles. This pterosaur, *Dimorphodon* (dye-MORE-fuh-don), lived in the Early Triassic. A meat-eater, it had large, sharp-toothed jaws that looked like a bird's beak. It had a wingspan of about four feet, and a long, pointy tail.

▲ "Beak Snout"

Some pterosaurs, such as *Dimorphodon* and this animal, *Rhamphorynchus* (RAM-fuh-RING-kus), had short necks. Others had long necks. *Rhamphorynchus* was a flying fish-eater of the late Jurassic. Its name means "beak snout."

▲ Wide Wings

Pteranodon (ter-AN-oh-don) had a body about the size of a modern-day turkey's, but its head and wings were huge. The head, including the crest and the long, toothless jaws, was six feet long. The wingspan was almost 30 feet from tip to tip.

GIANTS

Bigfoot!

Camarasaurus (KAM-uh-ruh-SORE-us) was huge—an adult was 30 to 60 feet long and 15 feet tall at the hips. This four-legged giant was a plant-eater. It had a small head, spoon-shaped teeth, a long slender neck, and a thick, powerful tail. Its bones have been found in North America and Europe.

This picture shows the huge feet of a *Camarasaurus* stepping toward you. (In the background is another *Camarasaurus*, standing sideways.) The *Compsognathus* (komp-sog-NAY-thus) running underfoot have no fear of being eaten. They are just trying to avoid being trampled!

▲ Treetop Titan

Brachiosaurus (BRAK-ee-oh-SORE-us) would have had no trouble peeking over the top of a four-story building. This megabeast was about 40 feet tall and more than 70 feet long, and may have weighed as much as 12 elephants.

"Earth-shaking Lizard" ▲

Without a complete skeleton, scientists can't be sure, but they estimate that *Seismosaurus* (SIZE-muh-SORE-us) was 130 to 170 feet long. That is about half the length of a football field! Most of that length was in this plant-eater's neck and tail.

GIANTS

Sticking Its Neck Out

The neck of *Mamenchisaurus* (mah-MEN-chih-SORE-us) puts it into the record books. It is the longest neck of any known animal: 36 feet—half of the animal's total body length. That neck was very flexible, thanks to its 19 vertebrae (bony segments). A giraffe's neck has only seven vertebrae, the same as a human's.

Holes in Its Head ▶

Diplodocus (dih-PLOH-duh-kus) had a huge body—about 90 feet long, including a 26-foot-long neck. Compared to that, its head was tiny—barely two feet long! *Diplodocus* had dull front teeth, no back teeth, and nostrils on the top of its head.

What's in a Name? ▼

In 1877, a scientist named Othniel C. Marsh was studying dinosaur fossils. He named the animal *Apatosaurus* (uh-PAT-uh-SORE-us)—"deceptive lizard." Two years later, he found fossils that seemed to belong to a different animal. He named that one *Brontosaurus* (BRON-tuh-SORE-us)—"thunder lizard." Once experts realized that the fossils were of the same type of dinosaur, they dropped the name *Brontosaurus*, although people continue to use it.

15

STEGOSAURS

Tough Guys

Like many herbivores, plant-eating dinosaurs had dull rather than sharp teeth. Such teeth were perfect for grinding up tough leaves, but not much help for self-defense against meat-eaters with sharp teeth and claws. Stegosaurs (STEG-uh-sores) were plant-eating dinosaurs with built-in defenses. They had very tough skin coupled with back plates or spikes. Some had all three. It was like a natural suit of armor!

As a hungry *Allosaurus* prepares to attack, a *Stegosaurus* gets its self-defense weapons ready: the four heavy spikes at the end of its tail. Each spike was nearly four feet long.

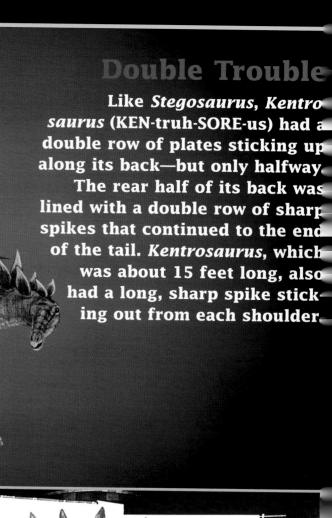

Double Trouble

Like *Stegosaurus, Kentro saurus* (KEN-truh-SORE-us) had a double row of plates sticking up along its back—but only halfway. The rear half of its back was lined with a double row of sharp spikes that continued to the end of the tail. *Kentrosaurus,* which was about 15 feet long, also had a long, sharp spike sticking out from each shoulder.

▲ No Brainiac

Tuojiangosaurus (too-oh-jee-ONG-oh-SORE-us) means "Tuo River lizard" and is named for the area in China where its skeletons have been found. Like other stegosaurs, it walked on all fours and had a large body with a small head—and a brain no bigger than a golf ball. *Tuojiangosaurus* was about 23 feet long and six feet tall, and lived about 155 million years ago.

◄ Cool Customer

Cryolophosaurus (KRY-uh-loh-fuh-SORE-us) was discovered in Antarctica in 1991. The name means "frozen ridge lizard" because it was found in frigid Antarctica and has a crest (ridge) on its head. When this 25-foot-long beast was on the prowl, Antarctica's climate was much warmer than it is today.

▼ Run, Dino, Run!

Elaphrosaurus (ee-LAFF-roh-SORE-us) had skinny arms and the long, lean legs and body of a swift runner. This dinosaur may have been an early relative of ornithomimids (OR-nith-oh-MY-midz)—birdlike dinosaurs of the Cretaceous period, which was millions of years later. *Elaphrosaurus*, which means "lightweight lizard," had another birdlike trait: lightweight bones.

▲ King of the Hill

Found mainly in Australia, North America, and East Africa, *Allosaurus* was the major meat-eater in its day. It fed on fellow dinosaurs, including iguanodonts and stegosaurs. The *Allosaurus* pictured above has taken a chunk out of a *Diplodocus* that could not outrun it.

Chicken Little

Compsognathus (komp-sog-NAY-thus) was one of the smallest dinosaurs known. It was no larger than a hen. It ran on two long birdlike legs, and had short arms. On each hand, it had two sharp-clawed long fingers and a stubby little one. It had sharp teeth, too—the sign of a carnivore. (Its name means "pretty jaw.") *Compsognathus* probably fed on small prey, such as insects, small reptiles, and small mammals.

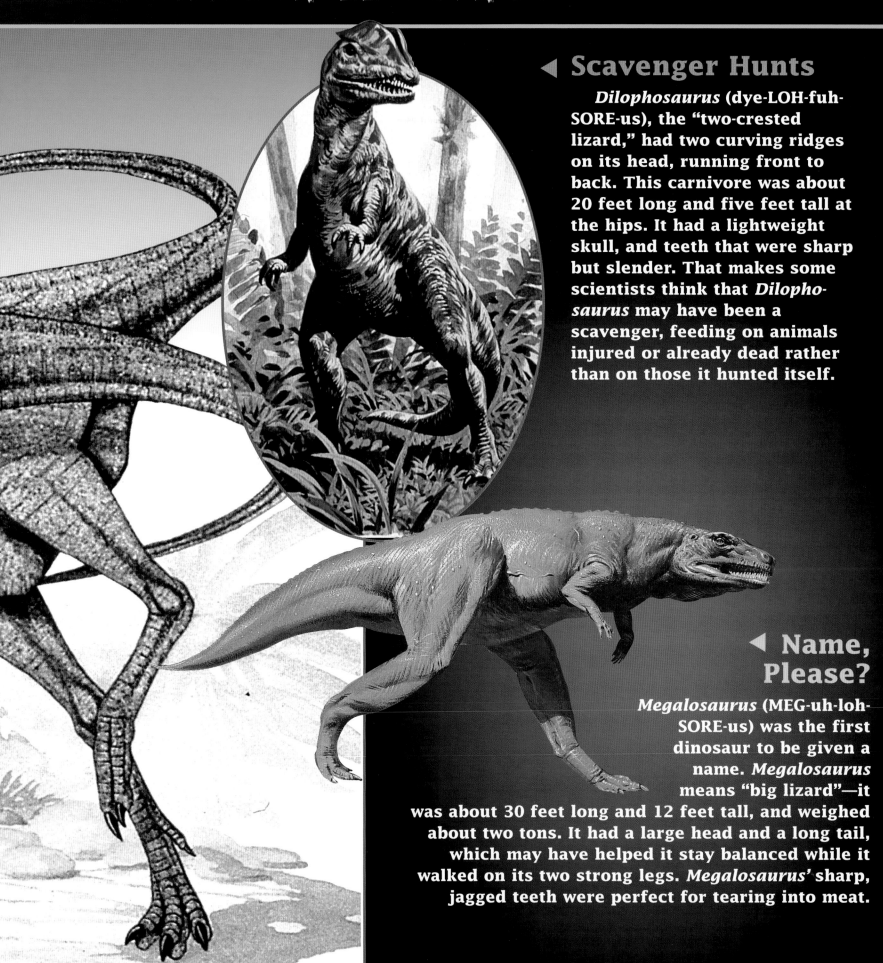

◀ Scavenger Hunts

Dilophosaurus (dye-LOH-fuh-SORE-us), the "two-crested lizard," had two curving ridges on its head, running front to back. This carnivore was about 20 feet long and five feet tall at the hips. It had a lightweight skull, and teeth that were sharp but slender. That makes some scientists think that *Dilophosaurus* may have been a scavenger, feeding on animals injured or already dead rather than on those it hunted itself.

◀ Name, Please?

Megalosaurus (MEG-uh-loh-SORE-us) was the first dinosaur to be given a name. *Megalosaurus* means "big lizard"—it was about 30 feet long and 12 feet tall, and weighed about two tons. It had a large head and a long tail, which may have helped it stay balanced while it walked on its two strong legs. *Megalosaurus'* sharp, jagged teeth were perfect for tearing into meat.

DINOBIRDS

▲ Taking Wing

The Jurassic dinosaur fossil above is world-famous for a good reason. It shows a small dinosaur with a meat-eater's teeth—and wings and feathers. *Archaeopteryx* (AR-kee-OP-ter-iks) is the oldest-known feathered animal. It may have used its wings for gliding on the wind rather than for flying. If it could truly fly, it probably could not have flown far.

Not Really Extinct ▼

Over millions of years, some dinosaurs developed features similar to those of modern birds—legs with three toes, lightweight bones, and a beaklike face—to name a few. No one knows for sure how dinosaurs became birds. This painting shows one idea of four giant leaps of evolution (left to right): *Compsognathus*, *Avimimus*, *Archaeopteryx*, and a modern-day pigeon.

What Am I? ▶

Confuciusornis (kon-FYOO-shuh-SORE-nus) fossils found in China show that this Cretaceous animal had the toothless beak and shortened, bony tail of a modern bird, but still had the claws of a carnivorous dinosaur. (In this picture, you can see those claws just inside the wings.) Some of its feathers were much longer than its body. *Confuciusornis* was the first known flying animal with a true beak (no teeth).

HADROSAURS

Face Facts

Hadrosaurs (HAD-ruh-sores) were a group of Cretaceous dinosaurs with a distinctive facial feature: a snout that resembled a duck's beak. There were different kinds of hadrosaurs (as shown in this picture). For instance, some had a crest on their head; some didn't. These gentle plant-eaters often moved in herds.

▼ Tending Her Nest

Scientists once thought that female dinosaurs laid their eggs, then left the young to fend for themselves. Fossils found in 1979 told a different story. Remains of a duckbilled dinosaur were found with her eggs, suggesting that she was a "good mother lizard"—*Maiasaura* (MY-uh-SORE-uh).

BONEHEADS

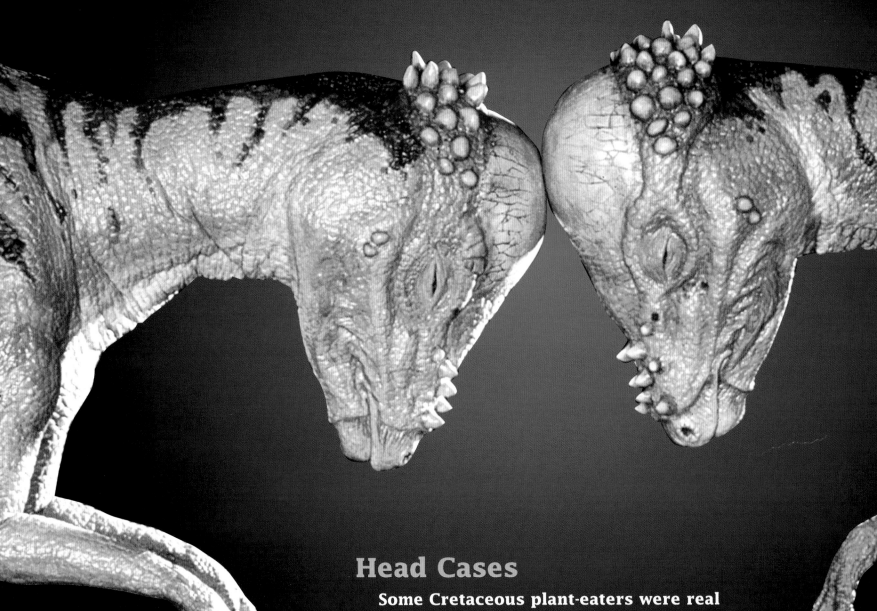

Head Cases

Some Cretaceous plant-eaters were real boneheads. A group of dinosaurs known as pachycephalosaurs (PAK-ee-SEF-uh-loh-sores) had unusually thick skulls. No one knows for sure why their brains needed all that protection. The males may have fought by butting their heads together, the way goats do. The group is named after the dinosaurs above, *Pachycephalosaurus* (PAK-ee-SEF-uh-loh-SORE-us), the "thick-headed lizard."

Self-defense? ▶

Besides having a thick skull, *Stygimoloch* (STIJ-uh-MOLL-uk) had bony knobs and lots of spikes on its head and face. The thick skull may have protected the brains of males when butting heads. The spikes were probably a defense against larger meat-eating dinosaurs. *Stygimoloch* was only seven to ten feet long. It lived in North America during the Late Cretaceous Period, about 68 to 65 million years ago.

◀ Thick, Thicker, Thickest

This dinosaur, *Stegoceras* (steg-OH-sur-us) had a frill, made up of bony knobs, encircling its head. The bone at the top of its dome-shaped skull was three inches thick. Some pachy-cephalosaur skulls were thicker. *Pachycephalosaurus*, whose 26-inch-long head was three times as long as *Stegoceras*'s, had a skull nine inches thick. (A human skull is only about a quarter of an inch thick.)

One glance at this dinosaur's tail should tell you that it was an ankylosaur. Besides some mean-looking spikes, *Euoplocephalus* (yoo-OP-luh-SEFF-uh-lus) was armored all over its body. Its armored eyelids could be shut like window shades to protect its eyes. No wonder it was named "well-armored head"!

A Tough Customer

Some Cretaceous herbivores had bodies built to keep large carnivores away. This family is known as Ankylosauria (an-KYE-low-SORE-ee-ah), which means "fused lizards." There were a few different groups, two of which were ankylosaurs and nodosaurs (NOH-doh-sores). Both had bodies covered with tough plates called osteoderms (AH-stee-oh-dermz). *Osteo* means "bone" and *derm* means "skin." An ankylosaur had a wide head and a tail that ended in a club. A nodosaur had a narrow head and a tail without a club.

Not on the Menu

Edmontonia (ED-mon-TOH-nee-uh), which grew to 25 feet in length, was the largest of the nodosaurs. With those fierce-looking spikes, *Edmontonia* didn't have to worry about becoming a meat-eater's next meal. Fossils of this animal were found near Edmonton, Canada.

A Mini Name

Minmi (min-MY) was a nodosaur. Besides some large body osteoderms, it had lots of small osteoderms protecting its belly. This plant-eater was named for the place in Australia where its remains were found. *Minmi* is the shortest of all dinosaur names.

CERATOPSIANS

Saving Face

Ceratopsians (SER-uh-TOP-see-uns) were a group of plant-eating dinosaurs that lived 145 to 65 million years ago. Their name means "horned face." These rhinoceros–like animals had bony horns and neck frills.

Triceratops (try-SER-uh-tops), at right, was 25 feet long and weighed more than an elephant. Its skull alone was more than six feet long! The name *Triceratops* means "three-horned face."

All Frills ▶

This is the skeleton of a *Triceratops*. One of the ways scientists can tell *Triceratops* apart from other ceratopsians is to look at the large bony frill at the back of its head. *Triceratops* was the only ceratopsian with no holes in its frill.

frill

▼ Fighting Off Attack

Styracosaurus (sty-RAK-uh-SORE-us) had a big head frill trimmed with dangerous-looking spikes, and another big spike on its snout. The spikes probably were for display or defense rather than for attack.

◀ Horn Free

Protoceratops (PROH-toh-SER-uh-tops) was smaller than its fellow ceratopsians. It was eight feet long and two feet tall at the shoulders, and weighed about 500 pounds. It had a neck frill, but no horns—just a sharp beak that produced a fierce bite.

HUNTERS

Going Sailing

Huge *Spinosaurus* (SPY-noh-SORE-us) had an interesting feature: a "sail" along its back. The sail was held up by spines up to 6.5 feet long, coming out of the animal's backbone. No one knows for sure what the sail was for. The extra skin surface may have helped this 40-foot-long meat-eater cool off when it was hot, and warm up when it was cold.

Going ▶ Fishing

The nickname "Claws" fits this carnivore to a *T*, and so does its real name. *Baryonyx* (BAYR-ee-ON-iks) means "heavy claw." This big beast—32 feet long and eight feet tall at the hips—had talons nearly one foot long. *Baryonyx* was an expert at spearing fish with its claws. It was efficient at eating them, too: In its long snout, it had twice as many teeth as other meat-eaters.

◀ Watch Your Back!

Acrocanthosaurus (AK-roh-KAN-thuh-SORE-us) had spines along its neck, back, and tail. *Acrocanthosaurus*'s sail was shorter, thicker, and tougher than *Spinosaurus*'s. The spines of this meat-eater's sail were attached to strong muscles. No one knows what this dinosaur's sail was for, either.

Bigfoot

A dromaeosaur (DROH-mee-uh-sore) is an animal that hunts using super-sharp claws. *Deinonychus* (dye-NON-ih-kus) means "terrible claw," which tells you how this dromaeosaur brought down its prey. Besides the usual sharp claws on its hands and feet, *Deinonychus* had an extra-long claw—up to five inches long—on the second toe of each foot. *Deinonychus* was about 10 feet long, but light for its size.

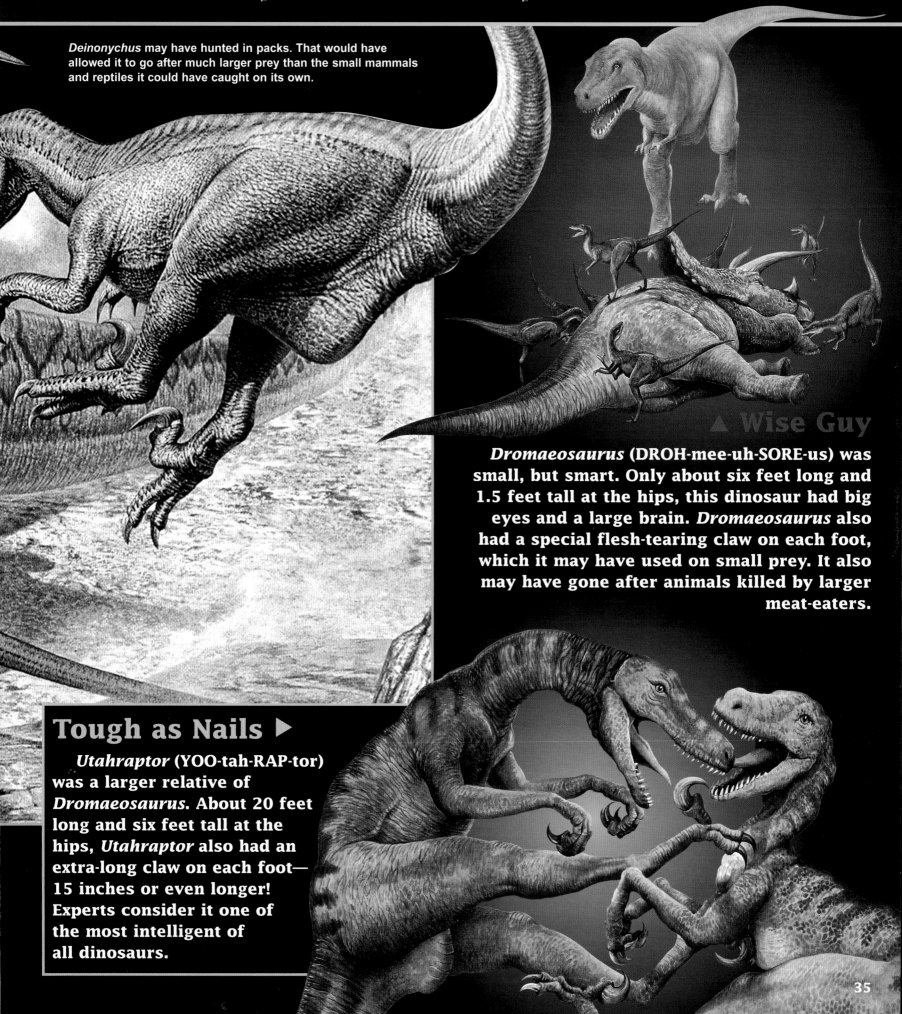

Deinonychus may have hunted in packs. That would have allowed it to go after much larger prey than the small mammals and reptiles it could have caught on its own.

▲ Wise Guy

Dromaeosaurus (DROH-mee-uh-SORE-us) was small, but smart. Only about six feet long and 1.5 feet tall at the hips, this dinosaur had big eyes and a large brain. *Dromaeosaurus* also had a special flesh-tearing claw on each foot, which it may have used on small prey. It also may have gone after animals killed by larger meat-eaters.

Tough as Nails ▶

Utahraptor (YOO-tah-RAP-tor) was a larger relative of *Dromaeosaurus*. About 20 feet long and six feet tall at the hips, *Utahraptor* also had an extra-long claw on each foot— 15 inches or even longer! Experts consider it one of the most intelligent of all dinosaurs.

TROODON

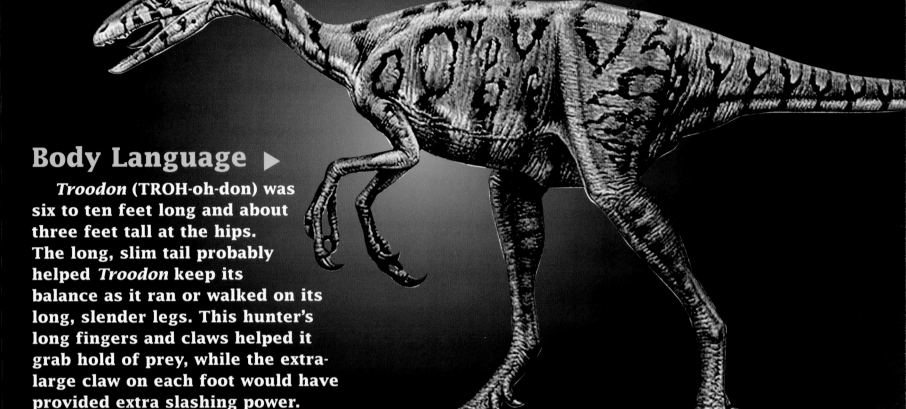

Body Language ▶

Troodon (TROH-oh-don) was six to ten feet long and about three feet tall at the hips. The long, slim tail probably helped *Troodon* keep its balance as it ran or walked on its long, slender legs. This hunter's long fingers and claws helped it grab hold of prey, while the extra-large claw on each foot would have provided extra slashing power.

◀ Gotcha!

Troodon was probably a swift runner—an advantage for a hunter. This *Troodon* should have no problem catching the fleeing *Orodromeus* (OR-oh-DROH-mee-us) nestlings.

Dino Einstein?

Troodon probably was one of the smartest dinosaurs. It had the largest brain in relation to body size of any dinosaur. However, *Troodon* was named, not for its brain, but for its many sharp teeth—the name means "wounding tooth." *Troo* is Greek for "to wound"; *don*, for "tooth."

OVIRAPTOPOSAURS

Mistaken Identity

Oviraptorosaur (OH-vee-rap-TORE-uh-sore) means "egg-thief lizard." When the first fossil of this kind of dinosaur was found, it was discovered with eggs. Thinking that the eggs belonged to a different animal, scientists thought that this meat-eater was stealing the eggs to eat.

Chirostenotes (KY-roh-sten-OH-teez) means "narrow hand." Besides those long, slender claws, this oviraptorosaur had a parrotlike head: a long, narrow, toothless snout with a crest.

◄ Heads Up!

Oviraptor was an oviraptorosaur. The crest on its head may have helped individual animals identify each other, or it may have been just for display. No one knows for sure.

On the Nest ▶

In 1993, scientists found another fossil of an adult oviraptorosaur above a nest of eggs. This time, though, the adult and the eggs were clearly the same type of animal. This fossil is of a mother *Citipati* (sit-uh-PAT-ee) with her own eggs.

BIRD MIMICS

For the Birds

A group of dinosaurs that scientists call ornithomimids (OR-nith-oh-MY-midz) lived in the Late Cretaceous Period. The name comes from two Greek words: *ornith*, meaning "bird," and *mimos*, meaning "imitator." The name "bird mimics" fits. Although they could not fly, these dinosaurs resembled some modern-day birds.

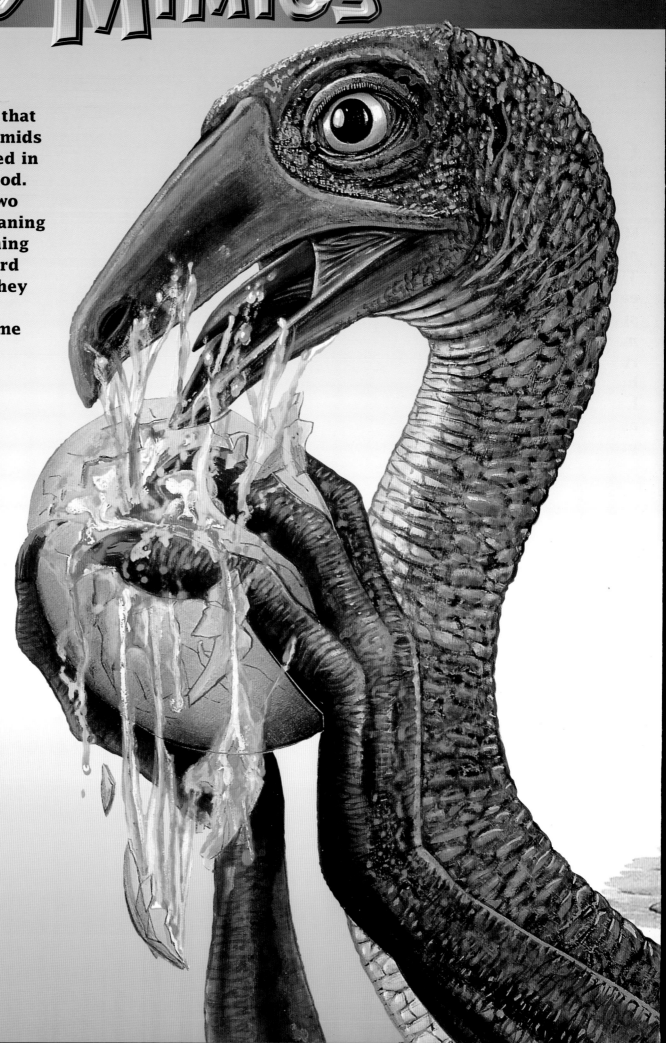

Gallimimus (GAL-ih-MY-mus) means "chicken mimic." At more than six feet in height and 13 to 20 feet long, this was the largest known of the bird-mimic dinosaurs. It probably was an omnivore—an animal that ate plants as well as meat.

40

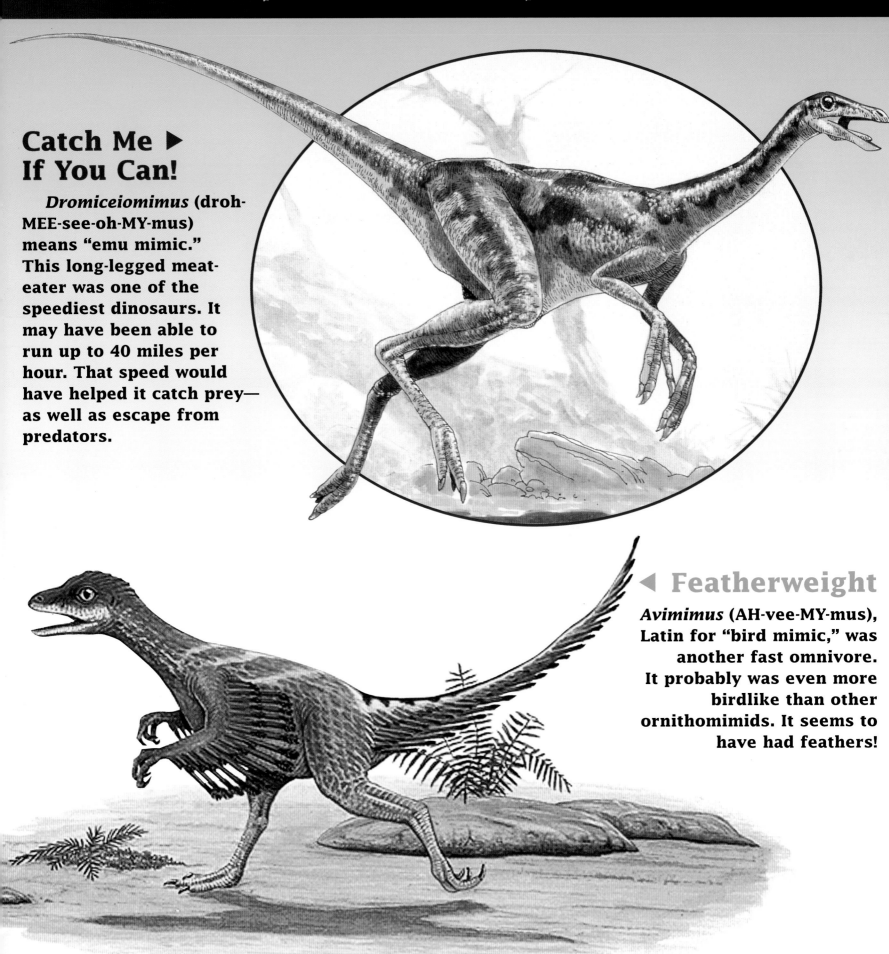

Catch Me ▶ If You Can!

Dromiceiomimus (droh-MEE-see-oh-MY-mus) means "emu mimic." This long-legged meat-eater was one of the speediest dinosaurs. It may have been able to run up to 40 miles per hour. That speed would have helped it catch prey—as well as escape from predators.

◀ Featherweight

Avimimus (AH-vee-MY-mus), Latin for "bird mimic," was another fast omnivore. It probably was even more birdlike than other ornithomimids. It seems to have had feathers!

41

Tyrannosaurus

As this *T. rex* mother grabs a *Corythosaurus* in her powerful jaws, she may have been teaching her young how to hunt for food.

▲ King of the Dinosaurs

Tyrannosaurids (tye-RAN-uh-SORE-idz) were massive meat-eaters. The name means "tyrant lizard," and it fits these fierce beasts. The most famous tyrannosaurid was *Tyrannosaurus rex* ("tyrant lizard king"). One of the largest known meat-eaters ever to walk on Earth, *Tyrannosaurus rex*—also known as *T. rex*—was 40 to 50 feet long.

Jaws of Death

Tyrannosaurus rex had a huge head. It was more than four feet long! The bones of its skull were several inches thick, giving extra crushing power to its mighty jaws.

Care for a Bite?

T. rex's teeth were an inch or more wide, and up to six inches long. They were curved and serrated, like steak knives. The many sharp edges helped this dinosaur slash through a large animal's flesh and bone in a single bite.

SEE THEM YOURSELF!

A skeleton of *Tarbosaurus bataar* being prepared for exhibition.

Get Up Close and Personal!

There are many places in the U.S. and throughout the world where you can see dinosaurs. Standing next to real skeletons and life-size models gives you a good idea of how huge some of these dinosaurs were.

◄ Various Views ►

A display at the American Museum of Natural History in New York City shows two views of a *Barosaurus* defending her young: a dramatic painting by John Gurche, and a mounted skeleton.

Take a Look

If you are traveling, check to see if there is a dino site where you will be. One place to look for dino sites in the U.S. and around the world is www.dinodatabase.com. (Click on the "Where to See Dinosaurs" link.) By the way, the *Coelophysis* that you met on page 8 is in this picture!

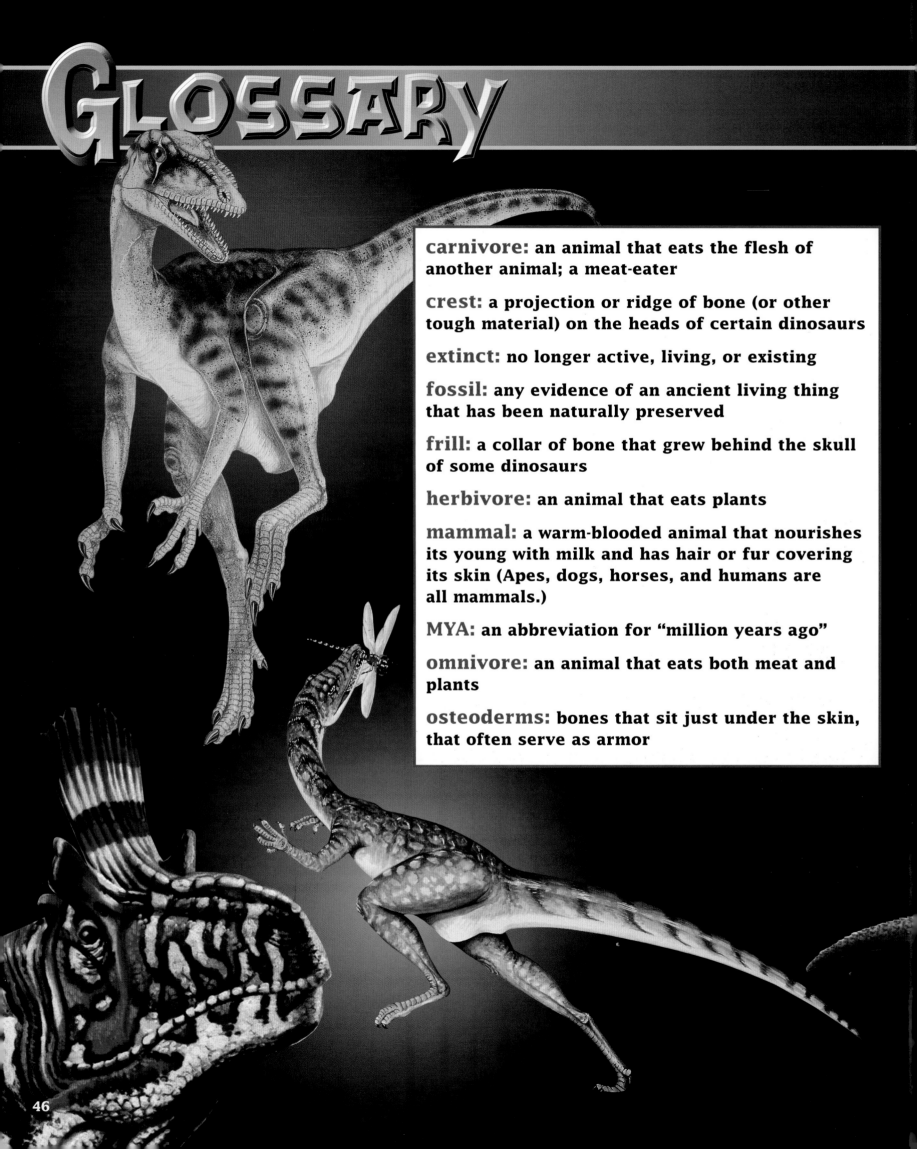

GLOSSARY

carnivore: an animal that eats the flesh of another animal; a meat-eater

crest: a projection or ridge of bone (or other tough material) on the heads of certain dinosaurs

extinct: no longer active, living, or existing

fossil: any evidence of an ancient living thing that has been naturally preserved

frill: a collar of bone that grew behind the skull of some dinosaurs

herbivore: an animal that eats plants

mammal: a warm-blooded animal that nourishes its young with milk and has hair or fur covering its skin (Apes, dogs, horses, and humans are all mammals.)

MYA: an abbreviation for "million years ago"

omnivore: an animal that eats both meat and plants

osteoderms: bones that sit just under the skin, that often serve as armor

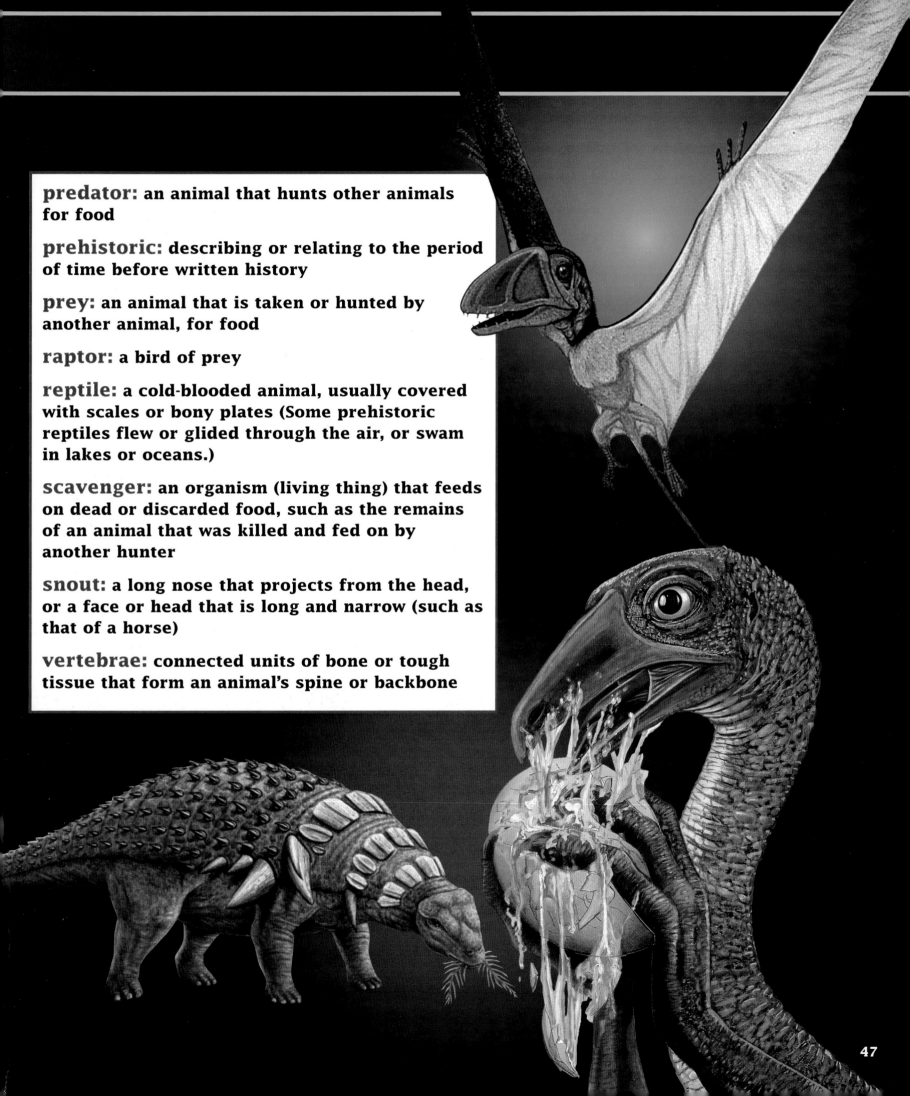

predator: an animal that hunts other animals for food

prehistoric: describing or relating to the period of time before written history

prey: an animal that is taken or hunted by another animal, for food

raptor: a bird of prey

reptile: a cold-blooded animal, usually covered with scales or bony plates (Some prehistoric reptiles flew or glided through the air, or swam in lakes or oceans.)

scavenger: an organism (living thing) that feeds on dead or discarded food, such as the remains of an animal that was killed and fed on by another hunter

snout: a long nose that projects from the head, or a face or head that is long and narrow (such as that of a horse)

vertebrae: connected units of bone or tough tissue that form an animal's spine or backbone

A movie-model version of *Velociraptor*, a Cretaceous-period dinosaur known for its large and very sharp claws